AF323967

A Crown for Gumecindo

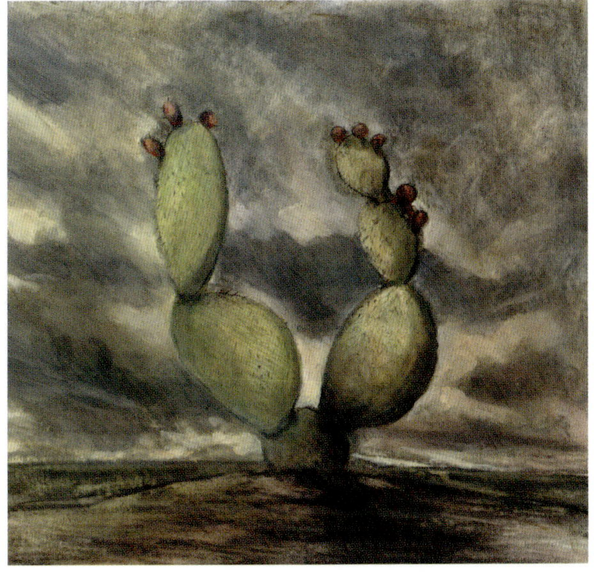

LAURIE ANN GUERRERO

PAINTINGS BY MACEO MONTOYA

AZTLAN LIBRE PRESS
SAN ANTONIO, TEXAS

Library of Congress Control Number: 2014956737

ISBN 978-0-9897782-2-0

1. Chicana/o Poetry 2. Mexican American Poetry

3. American Poetry 4. Sonnets 5. Heroic Crown of Sonnets

6. Texas Poetry 7. Tejano Poetry 8. San Antonio

For my grandfather

the first and greatest poet I knew

Gumecindo Martínez Guerrero

January 11, 1931– July 21, 2013

Foreword by Tim Z. Hernández

Names: Our names do more than simply make us accountable for the lives we live; equally important, they make others accountable. Particularly when our name is invoked long after we've left this physical realm. Our name is our connection to lineage; our past, present, and even future are all simultaneously present in our names. To say our name aloud is to declare ourselves alive. In Latin America, there is a call-and-response tradition that when the name of a fallen comrade is invoked in a public space, the entire community hollers back *¡Presente!* Which is to say, he or she is here with us now! Our names are the shining symbols of ourselves; they are our DNA in a string of letters. Our mothers can calm us or slay us depending on how they choose to say our name in a given moment. Friends refer to us by a nickname and suddenly we feel close, intimate. A teacher or authority figure mispronounces our name, uttering some indecipherable word we don't recognize, and just like that, we've been rendered invisible. So vital are these birth-given tags that, in some cases, people have been lost for decades, generations even, simply because their names were misspelled. Imagine that? Never having existed due to one seemingly insignificant oversight.

Which is why, when a poet decides to base an entire collection of poems on one name, that of a beloved grandfather, what that poet is declaring is, in essence, *I will rescue my beloved's name from the threat of obscurity, or the margins of history, and more importantly, I will offer his name, Gumecindo Martínez Guerrero, as a symbol for all the missing names in all the history books past and future.*

THE SONNETEER & THE ARTIST: Since the 1400's Italy's most revered sonneteers were employing this demanding poetic form, while nearby, its most influential painters were busily mastering the contrast between light and shadow, known poetically as chiaroscuro (chiaro - light; scuro - dark). In these early days, whether by sonnet or by paintbrush, the drive was to explore that elegant dance between two opposing forces, dark and light, life and death, love and loss, and perhaps question how both are necessary, vital even, in the illumination of one another.

In San Antonio's Poet Laureate Laurie Ann Guerrero's new collection of poetry, done in the key of the heroic crown of sonnets, no less, she revisits these origins, and simultaneously bends the possibilities. For the chiaroscuro that Guerrero's poetry renders in compelling language and form, the stark and visceral paintings of artist Maceo Montoya illustrates in bold images that alternately compliment or contrast the poet's subject. One thing that remains consistent between these two mediums: one always proves necessary in shedding light on the other. This dance between sonnet and painting, image and verse, coupled with the refined hand of craftsmanship from both artists, is what makes *A Crown for Gumecindo* a rare kind of gem. But why the sonnet?

In a recent interview, Guerrero spoke of her grandfather's craftsmanship as an influence as to why she chose this rigorous form:

> The sonnet itself became the only thing I knew was experienced enough to guide me through grief. The sonnet became for me a teacher, rigid mentor who expected my complete seriousness. In this way, the sonnet was very much like my grandpa: it expected me to work hard, to never give up, to be able to put my name, our name, proudly on something that was well-crafted, maybe even beautiful. But functional, always.

That the sonnet is typically comprised of fourteen lines, lends itself as an ideal medium for the subject at hand. There is something mythical at work here. Consider the Egyptian fable of Osiris who was ravished by his own brother and torn into fourteen parts, only to be gathered and reconstructed by his beloved, so that later, the number fourteen has a mythological association with death and reincarnation. In the same way, Guerrero builds with careful calculation a heroic crown of sonnets, that is, a cyclical pattern, a returning, if you will, where fourteen poems gain momentum toward one final, fifteenth poem—the reincarnation of her own beloved,

Gumecindo. Fragments of memory, dreamscapes, and conversations become the intricate gems that give the crown its sheen.

It is obvious that there is also an ethnography of grief at work here, where the poet investigates, using pragmatic tools, as well as heart tools, the life and death of her beloved grandfather, Gumecindo, who was at once a carpenter, woodworker and master craftsman. And of course, there is also the direct influence of the poet's muse. In the same interview, Guerrero recalled:

> When I would watch my grandfather in his workshop, he often left edges of a table, a bird house, a slab of sheetrock a little roughed up, never perfect. On the kitchen hutch he made for me of reclaimed wood, he left an emptied wasp's nest intact and attached: character, he said.

It takes a master craftswoman, and sheer boldness, to pull off a heroic crown of sonnets while at the same time bending the form. However, the poet's departure from the rules are not random or haphazard; the craftswoman respects, admires even, the traditional form. Likewise, with each careful verse she aims to elevate her grandfather's traditions, so that the cross-pollination of both lineages exists in a single breath. Beyond "boldness," what the poet is working through here is the urgency of her own grief, as she clearly lays out in the opening verse:

I wanted to take the shears to you: cut out the softened brain, the evaporating
bone. Do to you what I do to the poem.

With each word, each syllable, she is chipping away at memory the way a woodcarver might a tree trunk to reveal the hidden artifice within. The ruptures within the sonnets are a declaration of the poet's reverence for her grandfather, and his unique signature mark of leaving the wasp's nest as a way of inviting us to see through the myriad incarnations one life can take. In other words, the wasp's nest is there simply to remind us that before the kitchen hutch was an object functional for human use, it was once a home for other creatures. And before that, still, it was simply and majestically a tree. In the same way, before there was *A Crown for Gumecindo*, there was a craftsman and woodworker, a grandfather, as witnessed through the eyes of a granddaughter. And before that, still, there was simply and majestically a man.

INCANTATION: To say one's name aloud is to invoke their spirit and essence, is to counter the natural and supernatural forces that have had a hand in the demise of our beloved.

I look for your reflection in the mud,

Let me say your name again:

That oddity that was put in my hands.

Gumecindo.

Foreword

In the final poem, as we find ourselves chanting Gumecindo, the sonneto (little song) reveals its full incantatory power, akin to the way Mazatec poet-shaman María Sabina used word-songs to heal. Guerrero's verses elevate the name, Gumecindo, so that it intuitively becomes synonymous with ancestor/beloved/grandfather/sentient being/us. And only then, once we have summoned the man himself, we hear his own aged voice speak to us from the beyond: "Where else shall we live?" he asks. Indeed, where else shall we live, if not here, "together in ribs of the page," the poet answers.

El Paso, Texas
July 2014

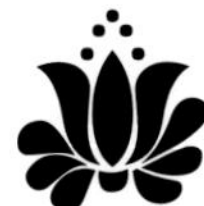

When I die, I want to be buried in a name,
some especially chosen, beautiful-sounding name,
so that its syllables will sing over my bones, near the sea.

–Pablo Neruda

I tried not to care anymore what your hammer built. What your truck carried. What you could see when you could see. The oil lamps stopped lighting the faces of the living. This is not living, you said. We were losing. We were too much for each other. I was no good for you and you were no good: they drew lines between us because you were forgetting, and I wrote things down, and this was no longer helpful: we were too much. We were too much for those who loved us. Didn't you know it'd be easier if you just got better? I wanted to take the shears to you: cut out the softened brain, the evaporating bone. Do to you what I do to the poem.

1. Where the Dead Come to Speak

El Paso, Texas/Ciudad Juárez

in this way
could she
–Valerie Martínez

And maybe there was a Laurie Ann who left

behind three children, a sink full of dishes,

a man who kissed her as if the whole world

lived in her mouth. And maybe, too, her heart

was carved out from underneath the cradle

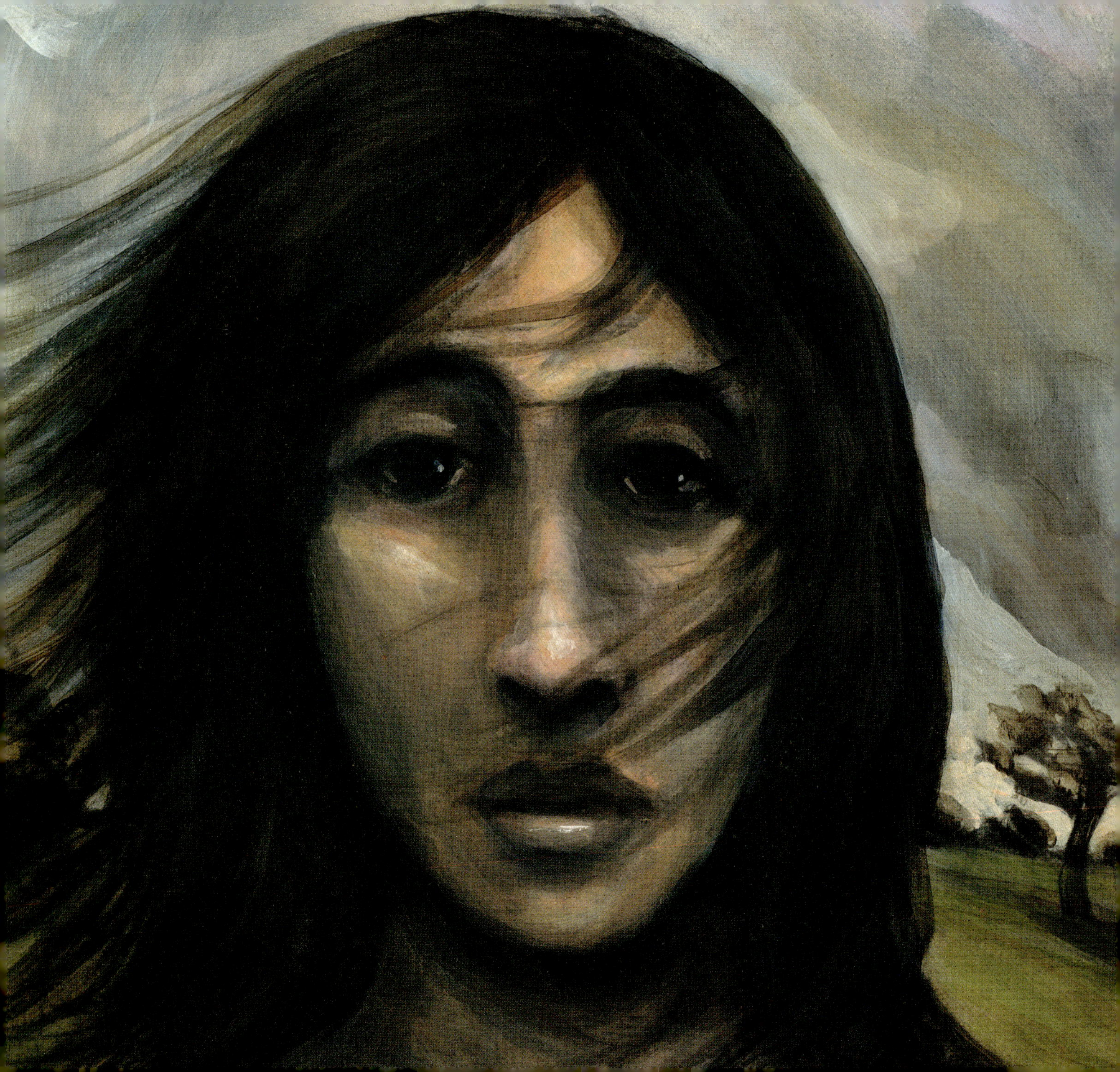

of her rib. The ocotillo motions

with its strange arms: death goes on. I conjure

you in bootsoles and sand, ice and humming

–bird, borderwalker and little girl.

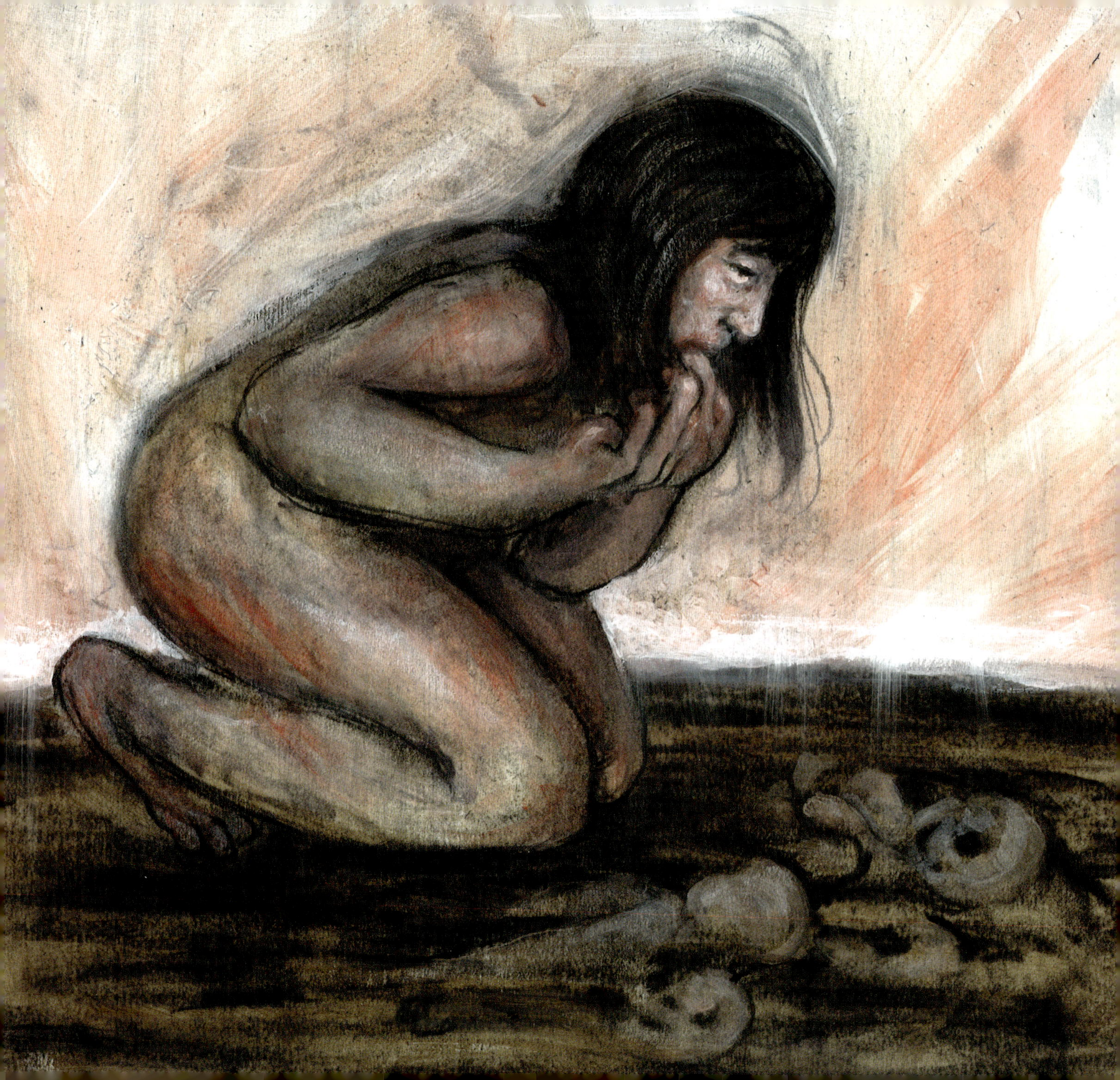

Have you found my likeness on the other side,

I memorized your hands when I was six years old.

as I search for you here? I thought you'd be

alone. You are not alone. Hadn't they

their own fathers to heed—saying, as mine

has said, don't be alone, don't cross the line?

2 Love is Our Mother

You said, don't be alone. Don't cross the line,

girl—the potential in my hands to raise hell,

you knew before I did. We were never good

but to each other: the brain creates

its devil: in this dream, he makes me choose

which of us will die by the hand of the other

and which of us will carry the dead home:

You kill the boy or the boy kills you, he says.

In this dream, my steady hands are not my own:

your hands load the gun: you know I cannot

let him live: his bones cannot hold the weight

of me. With my eyes, I see your hands. My eyes

see the boy I birthed—my jaw that quivers.

You wake me before you pull the trigger.

Are you sure? Are you sure? I want to know how you know if a person is dead. I held your hand, watched you take what I thought was your last breath, but what do I know? I've never seen a person die before, and what if I was wrong? And maybe, if we pull you up, you're gonna be pissed. What's wrong with you? you'll say to me like you do. What's wrong with you—putting me down there like that? You could've killed me. The obituary makes me nervous. What if I was wrong? What if I was wrong when I said, he's not breathing anymore? Maybe you were waiting. Maybe you were gathering your strength to say something, but they took you away, made me let go of your hand. And now you're in the paper and I've fooled everyone into thinking you're dead.

3. Praise Song for the Goat at the Grave

You woke me before you pulled the trigger-

tempting songs from your guitar—late night, after

cabrito plucked from its mother's body,

in praise of September rain: we ate. Praise

September, praise rain—though I can still taste

merciless July. At your grave, I nestle

hard candies in wet earth as to return

diamonds, as to sow seeds. I want your tongue

to wind its way through the hinged lip of casket,

black rock, pull them down to your softened teeth.

Who knows what you're capable of now—what grows

now that your heart has fed the dirt. But only

goats are here—bleating songs I do not know.

Only the goats are here to say hello.

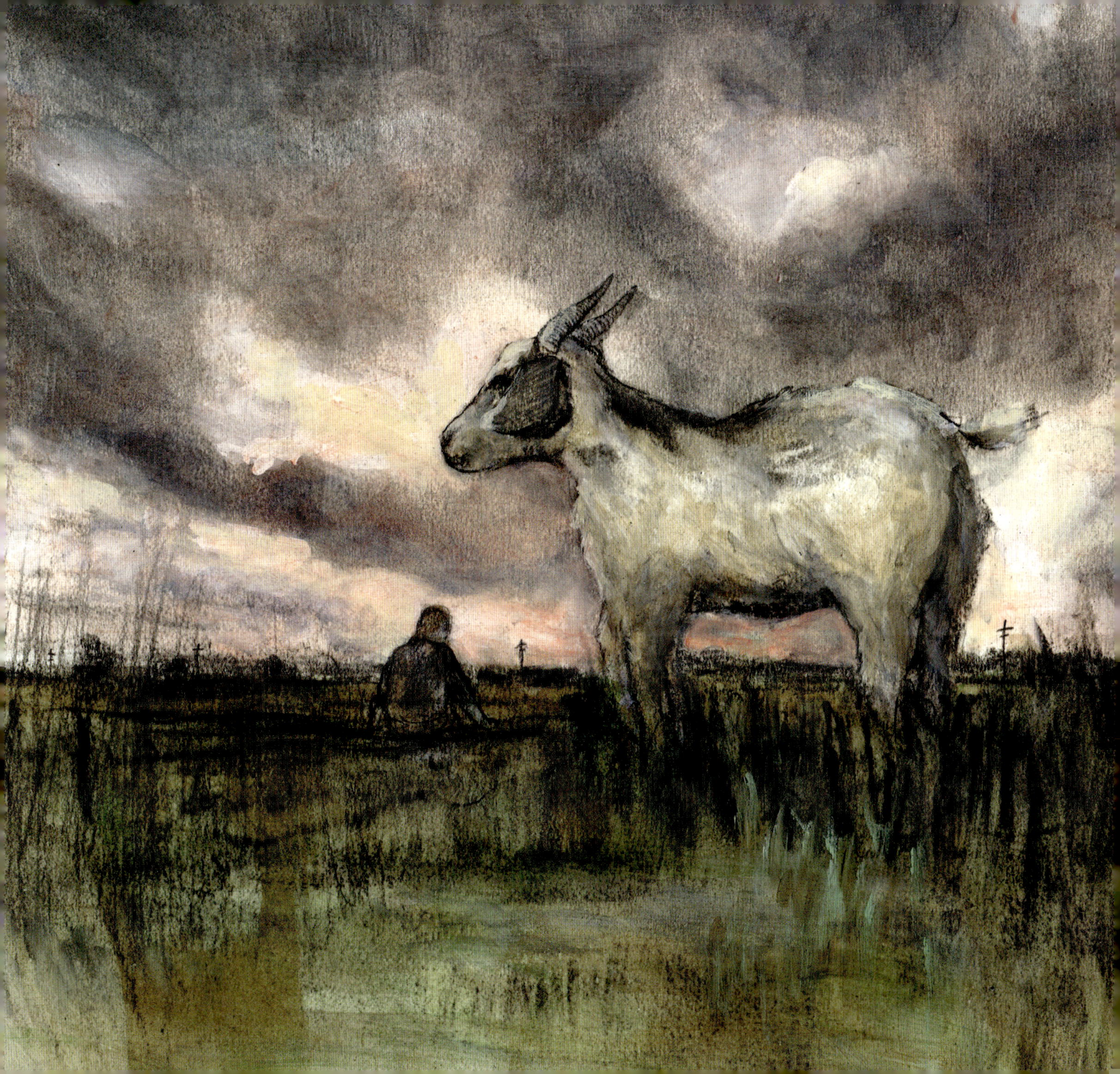

4. The Absence of Water

Only the goats are here to say hello

when I kneel at your grave. I straighten blue

ribbon from your casket, wipe dust settled

in plastic red roses: your headstone has

not arrived. I rearrange rocks, pull newborn

weeds that sprout like vocal chords: he's dead,

they hum. In my nails, your dirt burrows like worms.

My hands are dirty and you are not here

in your blue jeans, with your slow eye, to throw

me a manguera, to rinse my hands, to

wet my lips, to bless the little bodies

of tomatoes—trying to follow a sun

they can't see, shrinking, puckered on the vine,

shaking in their skins, faces split as mine.

Take me with you.

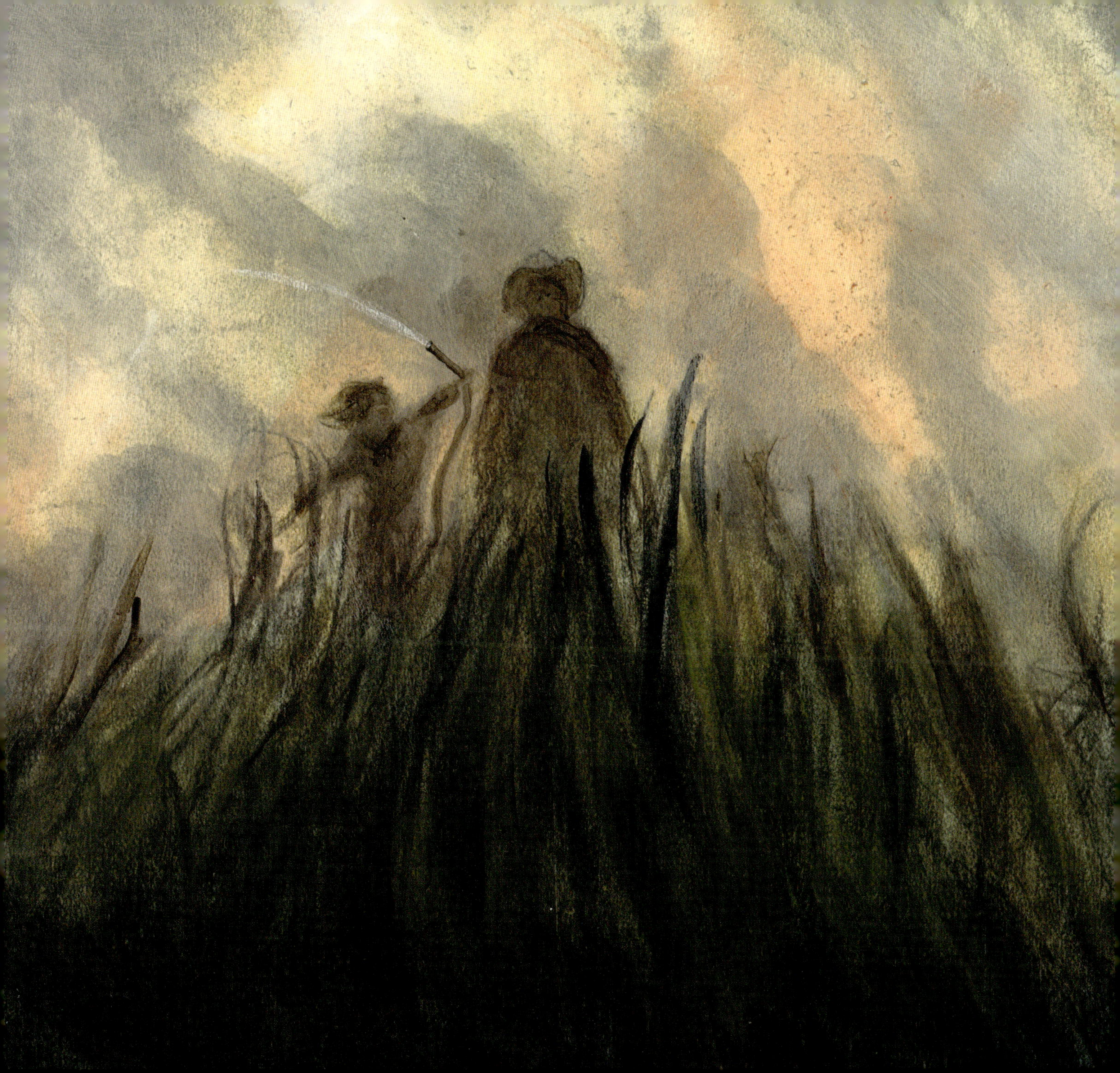

5. The Mesquite

Aching in their skins, faces split as mine,

the mesquite knows best: you died entirely

without me. There is a new kind of crying:

an untold red I have never known. Tears,

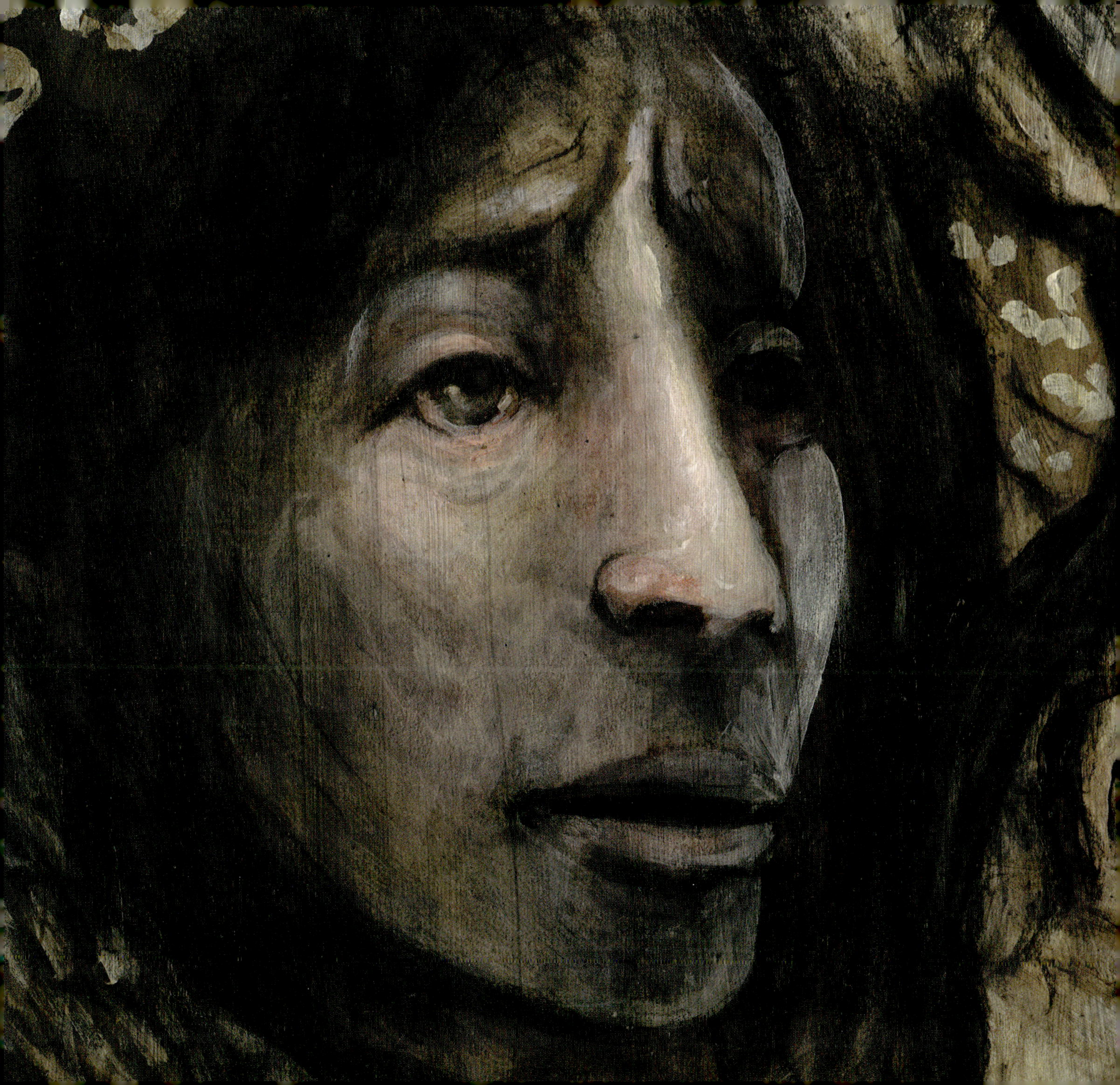

like mercury in the hollow of my

belly, like water burning through a well.

I hear the slosh as if I am a child

swollen with milk. In bed, I cradle my

own belly—ripe with an unnamed infant.

The mesquite separates us with his thin

finger. Before our births, he was coming

for us. I no longer love mesquite—his old

skin, his cold, brown face, tangled, and worn through—

like yours, mi muerto, the last time I saw you.

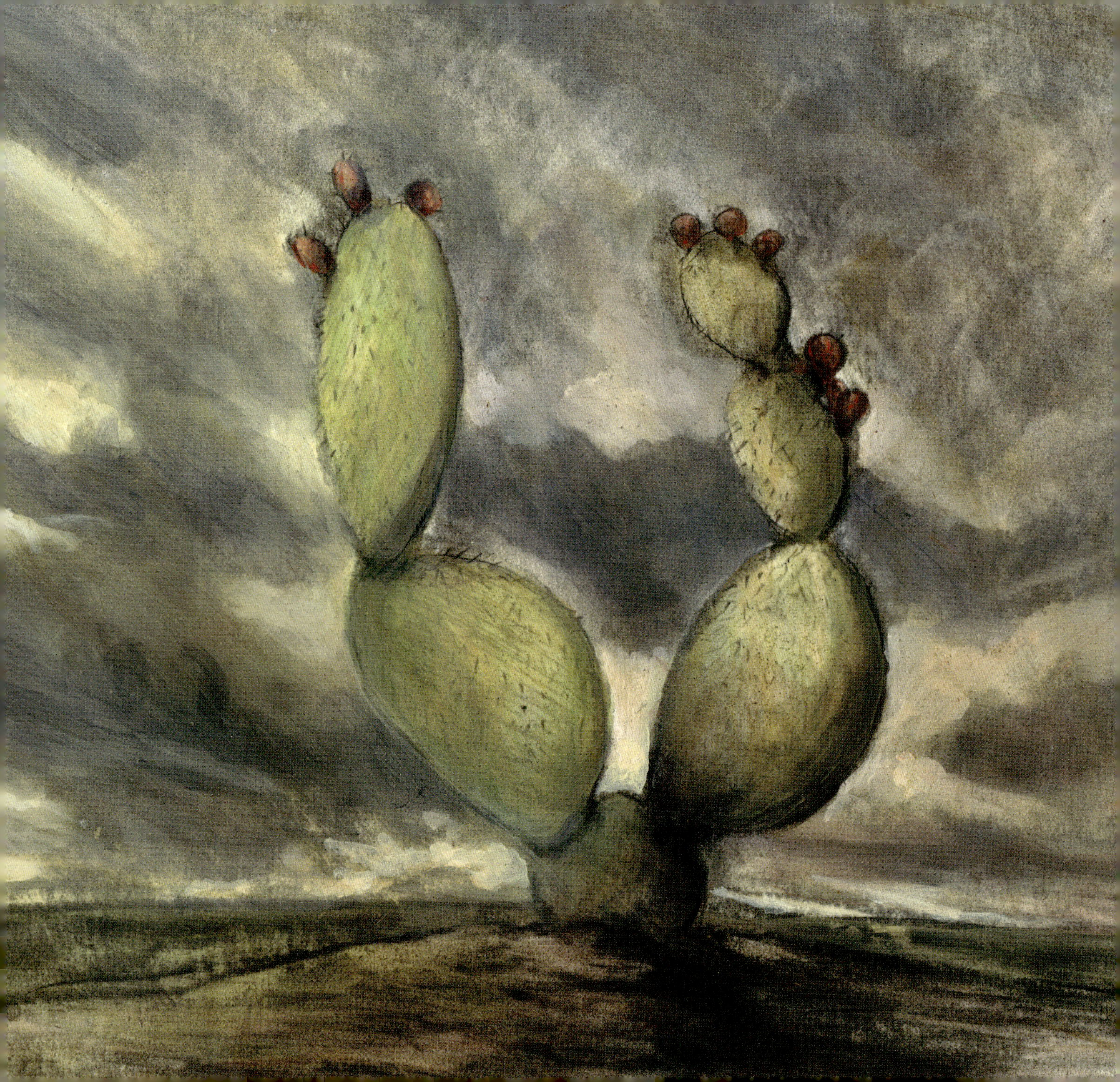

6. Without You I am Cactus

Like yours, mi muerto, the last time I saw you,

October's eyes are gray. Today, you are

not a dead man: October resurrects.

Today your blood, my blood, fills the private

rooms of my barbed and thorny limbs. I have

come to love October in the name of you.

Today, I say, you're back. Today, swallow rain.

Today, I soften on the earth; you emerge

from it. Today, I breathe life into your

dead lung. Today, I am God. Today, I

beat marrow into your bones. Today, yours

are the hands that pull spines from my spine.

Today, I shed my cactus skin for flood;

we'll look at our reflection in the mud.

2. *Newborns*

Let's look at our reflections in the mud:

see how, in four months, each of us has changed.

What is your name without a body? My name

without you here? I am new: what I never

was. Suddenly, I carry my newborn

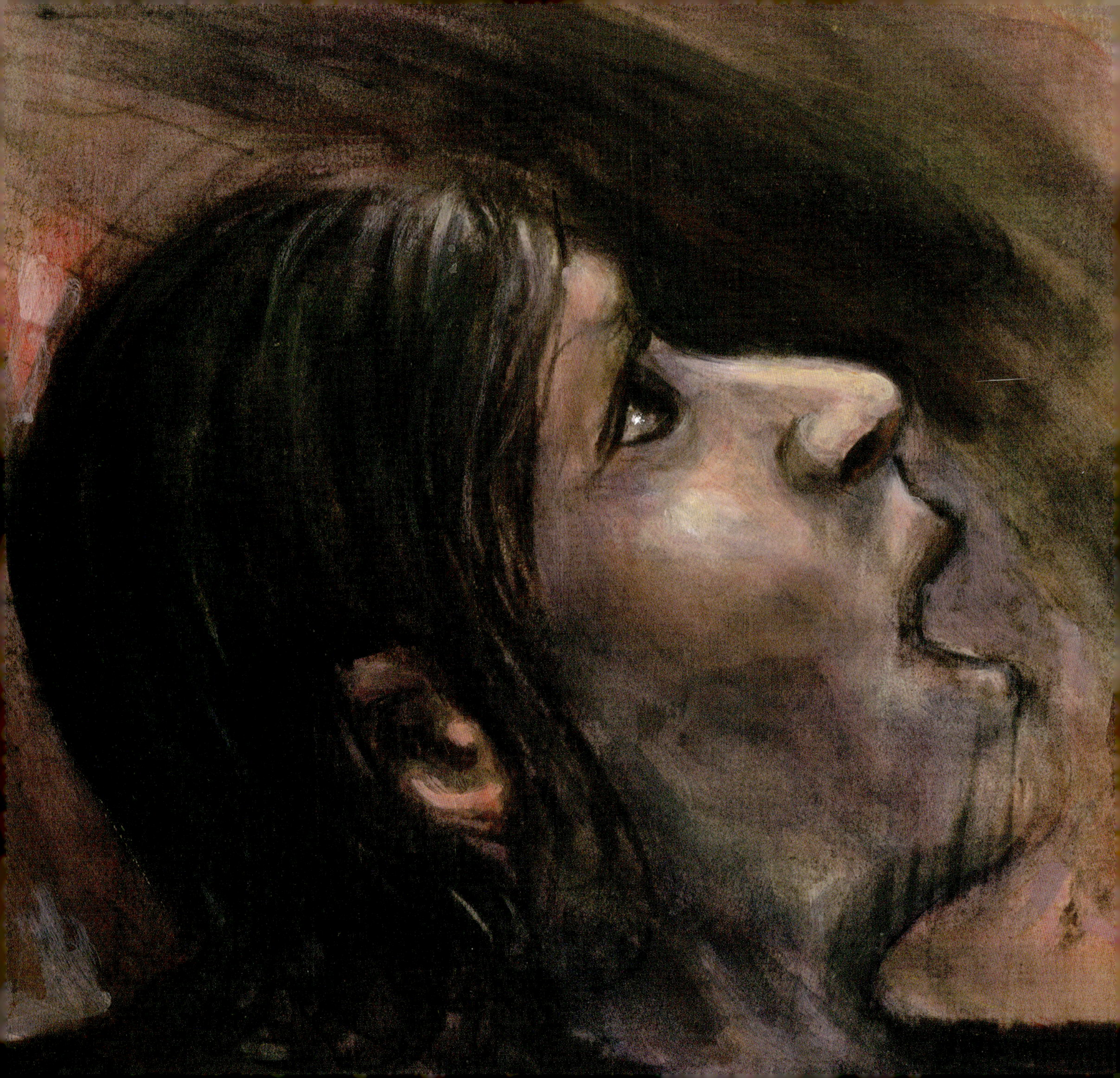

grief like a new mother—I nurse and swaddle

my most fragile, my newest, my sweet. What

festers in the bellies of strangers does not

concern me. There is only this: I am

the only mother. Mine is the only child.

I decompose alongside you, wanting

and not wanting everyone to see me—

off-balanced and leaking, my skin in strands—

the oddity that was put in my hands.

8. Día de los Muertos

El Carmen Cemetery, Bexar County, Texas

The oddity that was put in my hands—

your truck. It used to be I drove this road

each week to pick you up. Now I drive this road

each week to lay you down again. Today

is the day of the dead: When did you die?

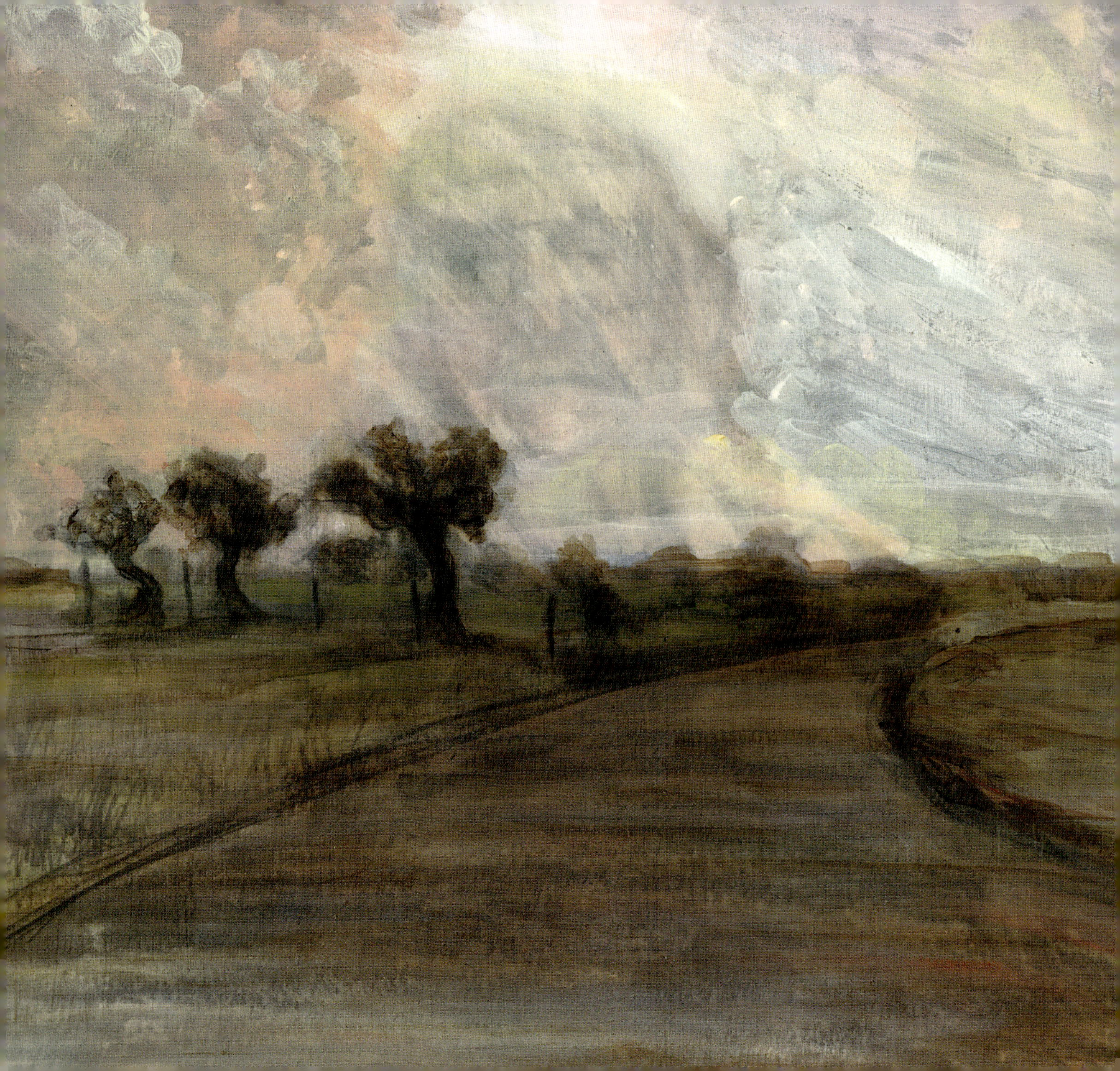

Today I bring you chicharrón con huevo,

chile. Which is to say, I brought breakfast

to the goats. I want to slip my hand into

the photo of you, fix your hair as I did,

help you with your sweater, guide heavy salt

to your plate. Grass is starting to grow over

you. Shards of rock gone smooth. I sing to bees.

I lay my ear to stone; it doesn't hurt:

I hear your song—water rising from dirt.

9. Sunday Dinner

I hear your song—water rising from the dirt

of Sunday. I peel potatoes for your

dead) mouth. I wear your teeth like an apron,

bandolier across my chest. I only

know how to feed you and fire. I think

I've lost my children, too. I look for you

in salt, in the red meat of sun. My children

are soldiers, lined rows of corn, ears wrapped in silks,

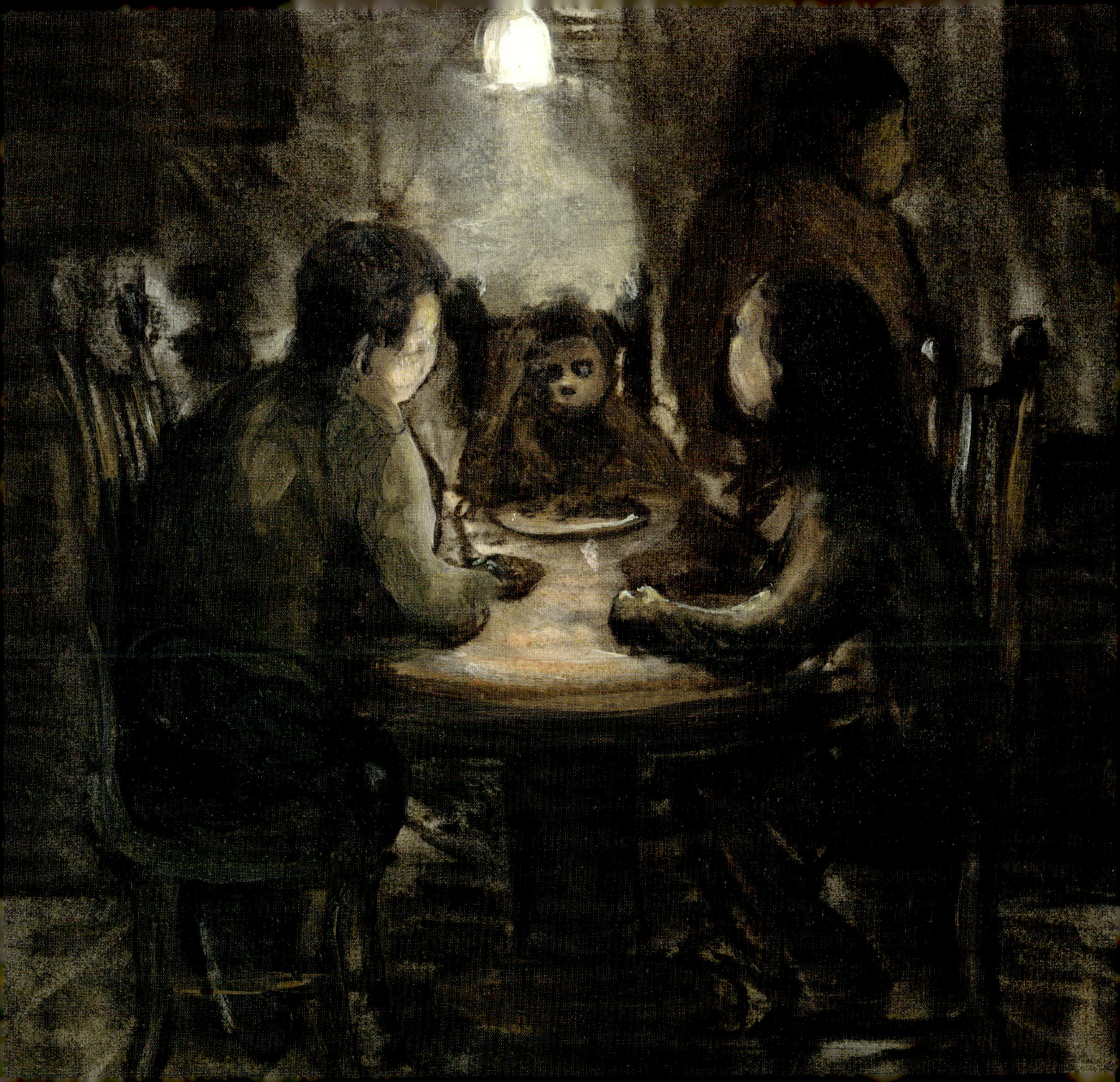

faces tucked in stalks. They have learned the war

of keeping: we trudge through the mud of Sunday.

At the table, we take from each other's

What was the name of ... (you are dead).
I can bring you pan dulce (you are dead).

faces—little fires. When you were here,

I didn't know to serve the meal this way.

Good? I would ask. Good enough, you would say.

(You are dead.)

But maybe you aren't.
Maybe you'll say,

What's wrong with you?

I'm sorry, I thought you were dead.

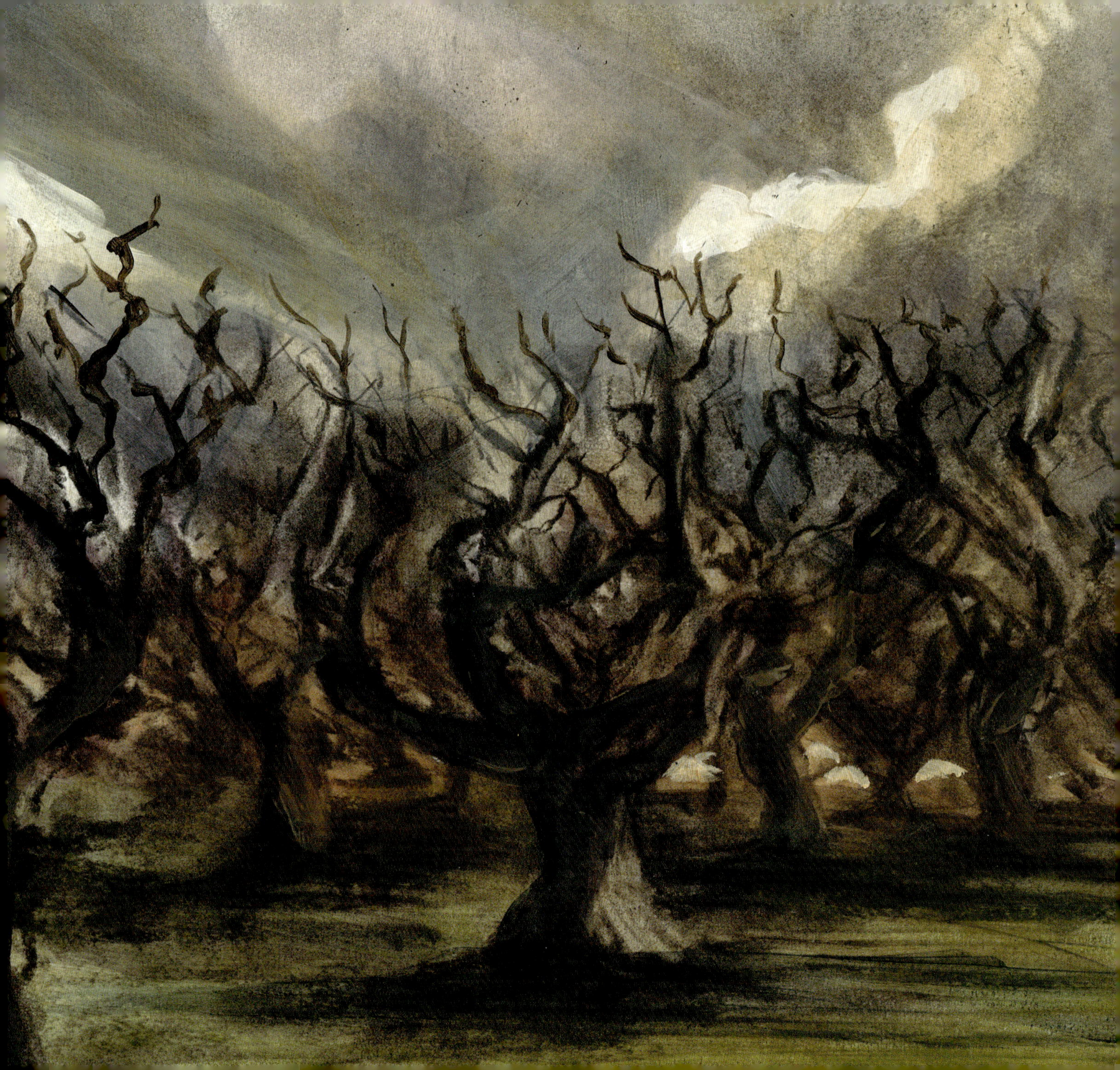

10. *Stone Fruit*

Good? I would ask. Good enough, you would say

of the wine we made from plums. Didn't we,

for years, tend the mothertree? Didn't we,

for years prune, pluck, hold in our hands the purpled

bodies bursting, that begged: me next, have me?

Weren't we so nourished in the nerve? Someone

is buying our tree. You are reduced to pit.

I put seed in dirt, wait for you to come

back to me in a jar by the window.

You are not growing. Aren't you a plum?

Little red, little kidney, little mouth

singing, calling: I'm here! I'm here! I thought

the dirt would give you something to take hold of:

I've buried everything I've ever loved.

I wait every day and every night to see you. Maybe you will come. Maybe I will walk into my studio, and your good hat that rests on top of the hutch you made for me will be gone, and I will look around the room looking for the hat, and you will be there, maybe, translucent, maybe glowing, but with dirt on your shirt and hands, the way you were, the way you have always been. And you will smell like yourself—sawdust and sweat and dirt. And you will hug me with your translucent, glowing arms, and I won't be scared because it's you, and I'm the only one you trust. How many times did you say that to me? How many times?

You don't come. Strange things, though: big brown goats one week after you died at your grave. A rooster in the drive-thru at the taquería where I bought your tacos. Cardinals when I'm thinking of you, hummingbirds when I'm not, and lady bugs on my books, inside, like I am a meadow and this is a fairy tale.

But I only want to see the strange animal of your face. How I try to look like you when I am in the mirror. But you don't come.

11. *Casketing*

I've buried everything I've ever loved

in the bone of reason: now, even in dreams

you are dead. Sometimes, I wheel your metal-

colored coffin to the grocery store.

Once, to a paperie. Twice to Fiesta

Bakery on Pleasanton. You are heavy.

Once, I was in high school, in a play, and parked

you stage left. Always, I shake you: *Wake up,*

damn you. Sometimes, the casket is open

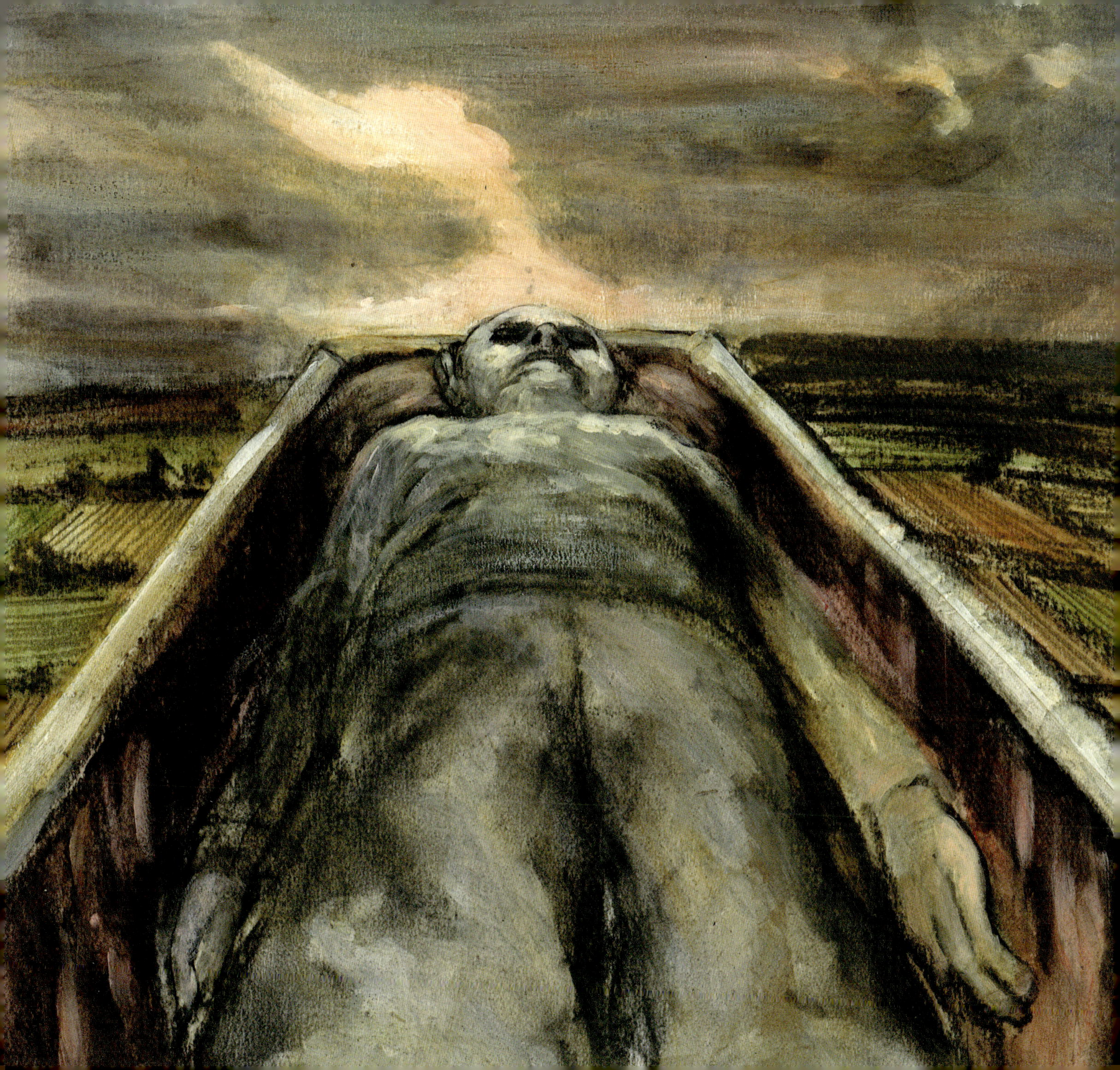

and I kick you. And when, in my small shoes,

I make contact, your ribs crumble like the bark

of an old mesquite: *Wake up, wake up!* We can't

run the numbers, argue, make your mother's bread

if you are always going to be dead.

I want to build you a house where we can sit:
me with my brown hair, you with your dead hands.

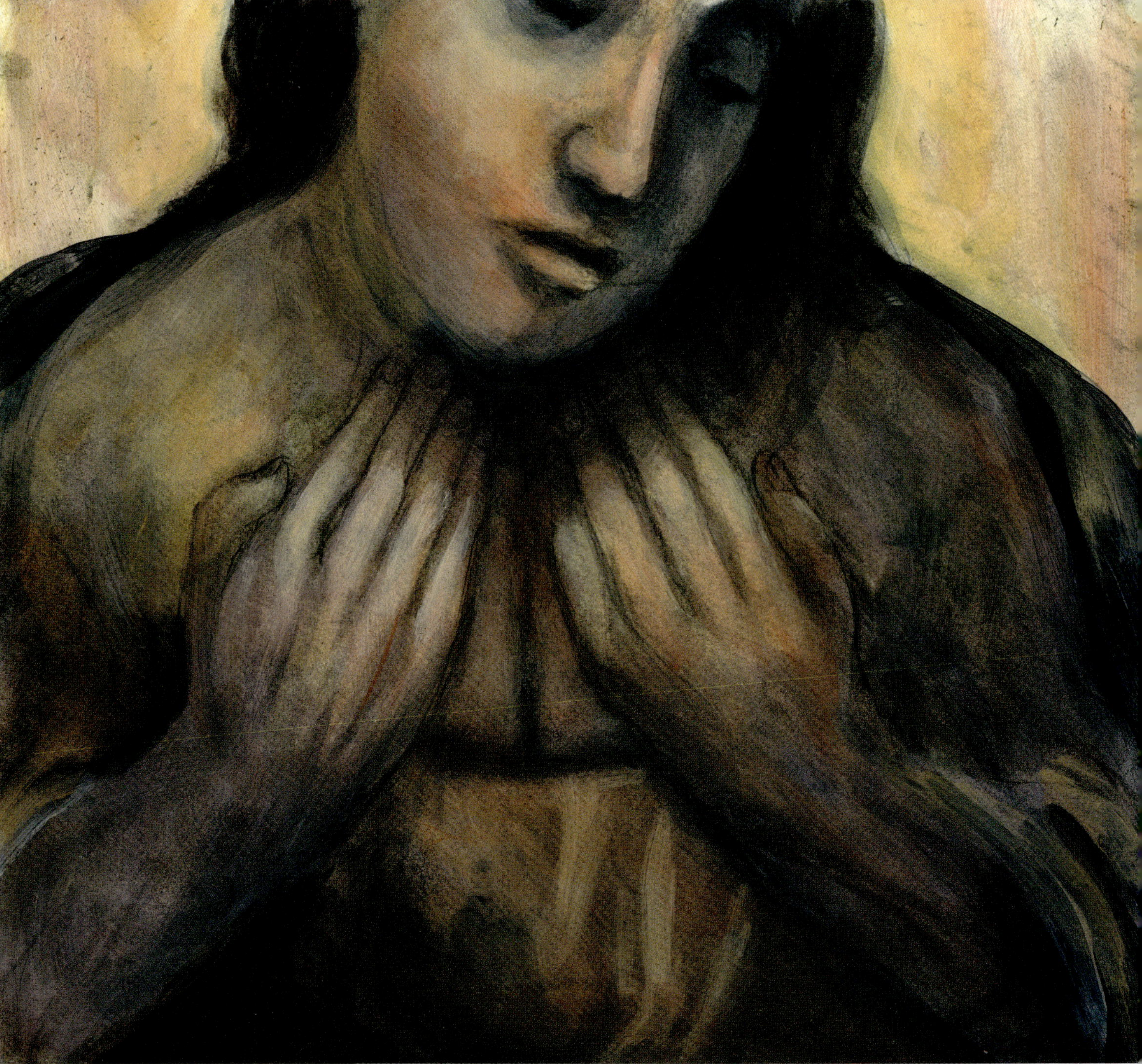

12 Untouchable

If you are always going to be dead,

who then will melt away the breasts from my

chest? Need more my eyes than the unraveling

of my hips? In your house, I was all bedrock

and teeth. Cutthroat. Stopped clock—just as much man

as woman. Or rain. You were blind and I loved

you for it. In your house, my shoulders grew

to fit the work. Patience blossomed upon

my head: a crown. You were my mirror: my name,

ready plum of my right hand, my ancient

and river'd neck, my compass, my wing, my

open gate, my warrior, my sleepless legion—

as if I had been born male: my kingdom come.

And one day in hot July, my kingdom gone.

13. The Work: Blueprints for the Body

One day in hot July, my king, you were gone—

wheeled out under the red and early sky.

Until you find me, I build a house: carve

boulders with your chisel, sweep fire and air

aside with sage, dig tunnels with my hands.

What are you preparing for? they ask. I keep

working. If a dog in my path bares his teeth,

I eat him whole. Ten months in, I am almost

done: stones are flat. I've mastered the level,

T-square, carved my own name in the handle

of my own hammer. A spider returns

to the center of her web—how will you come?

Muscle or rain? I have, 'til you come down,

only the page from which to build this crown.

I dream a room with small cows. Your youngest grandson and I wipe the snow from their tiny hides. They fit in the palms of our hands. We rub clean their hooves, their tails like thread. When I pile them into a nest, little black and white bovine, they are rats. I try to hide my shock, my disgust. I need to find the answer. What is the question?

Finally, in a country store, I see a man with a beard. A cowboy. His long legs lead me to a hall. I know him. He is my uncle, dead one year. In a room, he is sitting on a bed: Mija, he says, what is your question?

Uncle, I say, I am so sad.

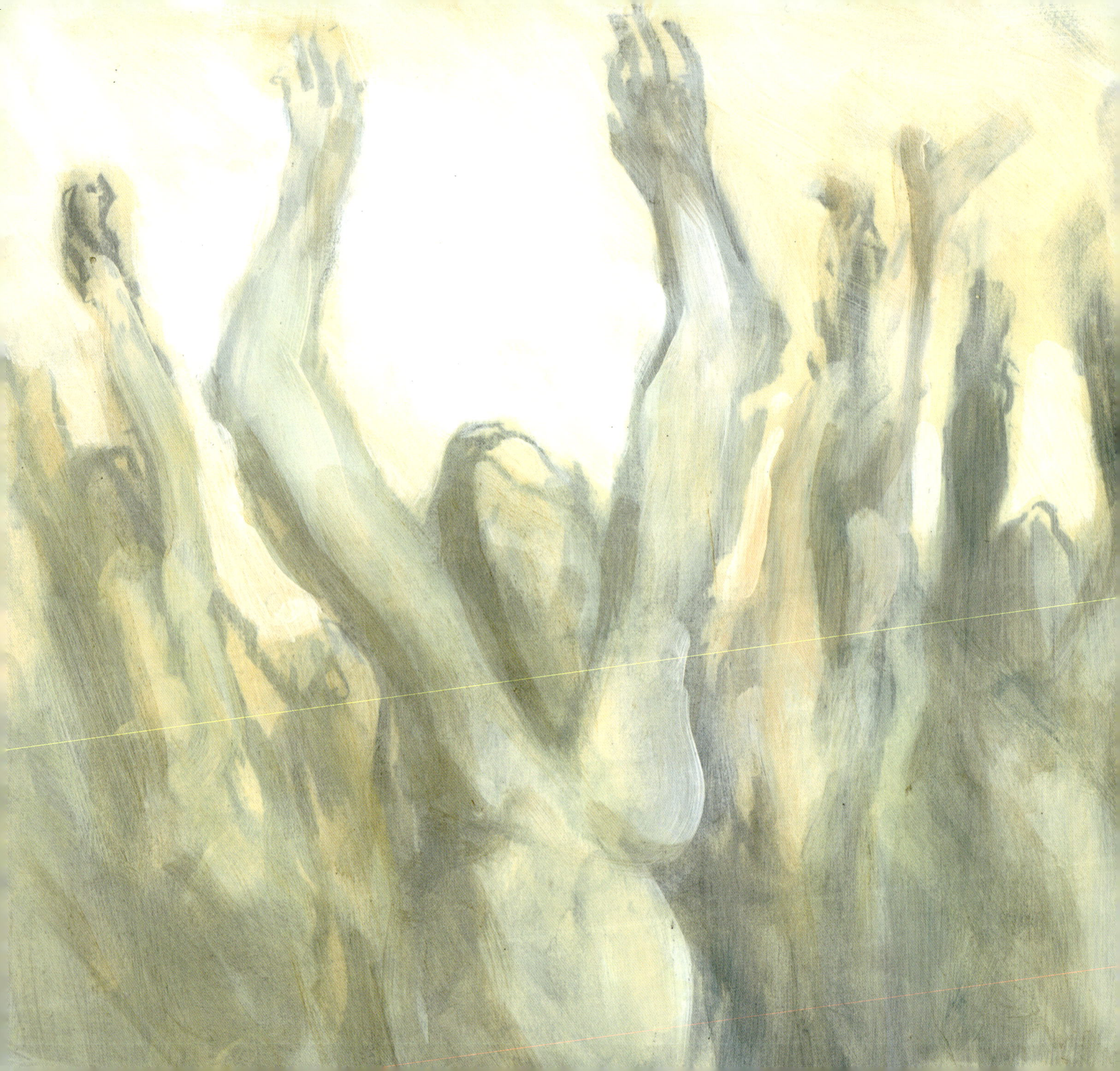

14. En las Costillas de la Página

Only the page on which to place your crown—

No one will need to know how old you were
when you learned to write

ink-soaked reliquary: here goes your hat,

your name.

your skin, my love, my Gumecindo. Grandpa,

meet me here all my life. Let us gather

together in the ribs of the page—I will

bare myself in the soft curve of your name.

I will loosen, unbolt hinges from my nape.

Let spill the garden you would have me tend:

praise the perfect hand of each artist, each

perfect work, each perfect loss in every field

we know or do not know; mark the unringed

finger of your left hand, speak names unspoken—

the pulling apart of one from another.

Let the record be the muse for the craft:

Where else will we live, Laurie Ann? What's left?

I feared this day would come:
only two times I thought of you.

Which one of us is failing?

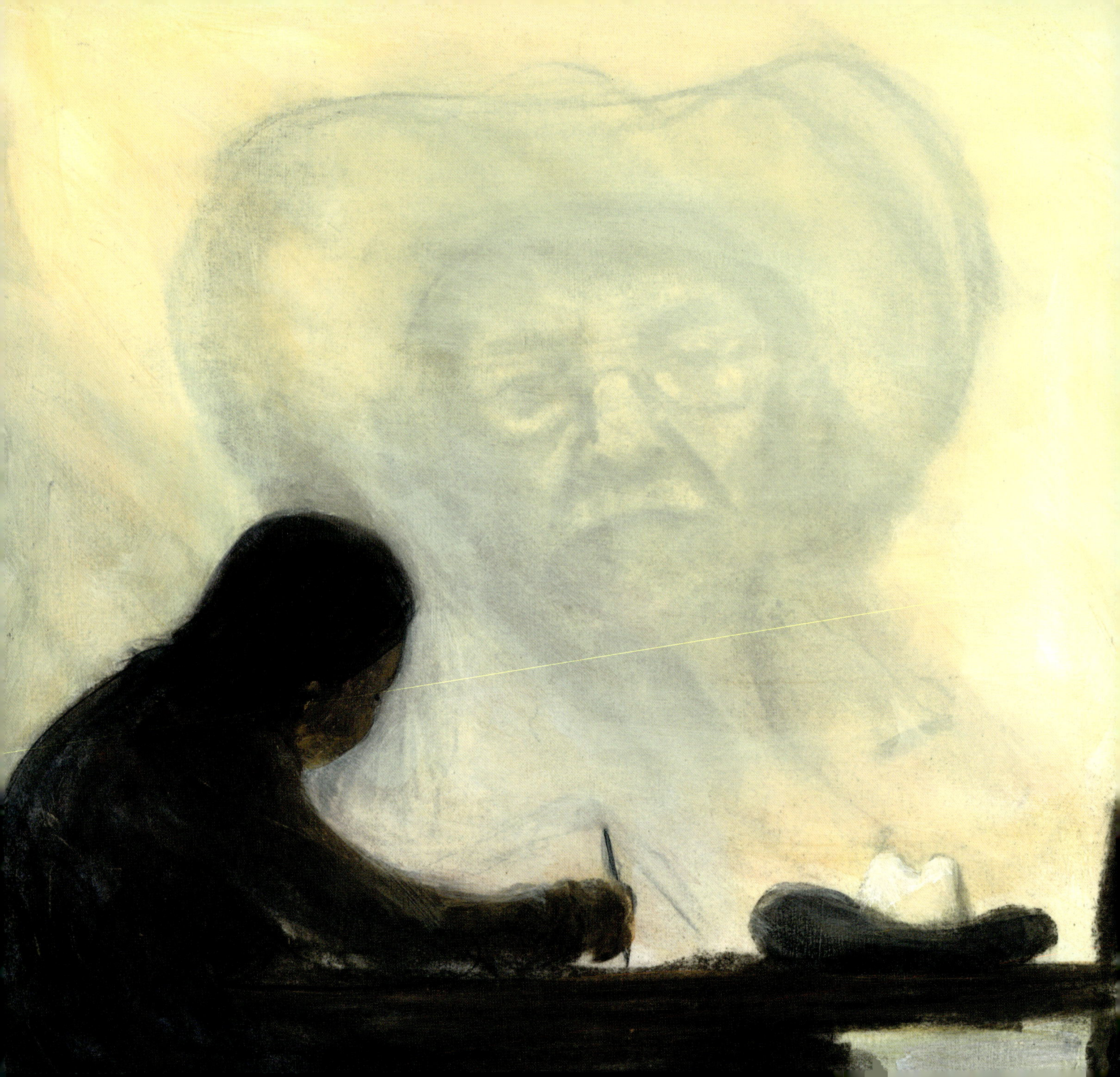

15. Goodbye Sonnet

And yes, I am the Laurie Ann you left,

who begged: Don't go alone. Don't cross the line.

Aren't you a plum?

I've learned to keep my finger off the trigger,

How many times did you say
that to me? How many times?

spare the goats who've come to say hello,

shaking in their skins, faces split like mine—

like yours, mi muerto, the last time I saw you

sing.

I look for your reflection in the mud,

that oddity that was put in my hands.

Gumecindo.

I hear your song—water rising from dirt:

Good? I ask. Good enough, you say.

I've buried everything I've ever loved:

        Gumecindo

You are always going to be dead.

        I sing to bees:
        Gumecindo
        Gumecindo

One day in hot July: my king you were gone—

only the page on which to place your crown.

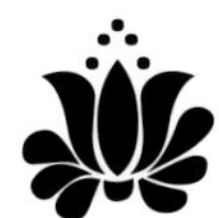

I visited El Paso for the first time shortly after my grandfather's death. I fell in love with the Ocotillo, a cactus I was unfamiliar with. Because of the femicide that has taken place in Cuidad Juárez in recent years, I did not visit that city. But Juárez was so close—in geography and in spirit. It was as if each loss on the other side of the border magnified each loss on this side. Not understanding my own movement through grief, El Paso offered a space for me to explore it. For the first time since I had lost my grandfather, I felt that there were people around me who knew what I knew—more so: knew a kind of loss that I could not fathom. I found myself wanting to pull their stories out of them, but I hadn't the strength nor the right. I knew, then, writing about grief—however challenging—mine would never compare to theirs. But I knew, too, that, as a woman, a living woman, I had been brought to that border place to contemplate both sides, to feel the grief in the air, to feel at home, to understand that like the Ocotillo, there were many things I would not be familiar with and that they would exist regardless—with or without me—tragic death, natural death. I could only have understood this in El Paso. And it was there that I started to understand what it meant to mourn. I started these sonnets there.

The book's epigraph is borrowed from Pablo Neruda's *Confieso que he vivido: Memorias* (Farrar, Strauss and Giroux, 2001).

The epigraph in the first sonnet is taken from Valerie Martínez's *Each and Her* (University of Arizona Press, 2010), a book-length poem about the Juárez murders.

The title of sonnet #2, "Love is Our Mother," is borrowed from Rumi's "Whispers of the Beloved."

The line, "you died entirely without me," in sonnet #5 is borrowed from Edward Vidaurri's "Calaveras: Day of the Dead."

Maceo Montoya's 15 paintings (acrylic and charcoal on paper, 2014) were produced specifically in response to the 15 sonnets.

Acknowledgments

Thanks to the editors of the following publications for sharing earlier versions of this work: "Without You I am Cactus," "Newborns," "Día de Los Muertos" in *Borderlands: Texas Poetry Review*; "Sunday Dinner," "Stone Fruit" in *Luna Luna*; "Casketing," "Untouchable" in *Cobalt Review*; "Praise Song for the Goat at the Grave," "The Absence of Water," and "The Mesquite" in *San Antonio Express-News*.

And for your sharp eyes and gentle hands during the building of this crown, thank you, Carmen Tafolla, Norma Cantú, Lauren Espinoza, Dan Vera, Yndalecio Isaac Hinojosa, Candace de León-Zepeda, Aracelis Girmay, ire'ne lara silva, Benjamin Alire Sáenz, Martín Espada, Joan Larkin, Mauricio Rodríguez, Margie Rodríguez, Juan Luís Guzmán, Natalia Treviño, Macarena Hernández, Ito Romo, Anthony Flores, Rich Villar, Ryan Sharp, M. Paul López, Barbara Renaud González, Sheila Black, Gerard Robledo, Anisa Onofre, Juan Tejeda, Kendra Colburn, Xelena González, and grandpa's most devoted sisters, Minerva Sandoval & Julia Ornelas.

Very special thank you, Tim Z. Hernández, for our good talks about grandpas & work & writing, for honoring our ancestors in these pages & in your own and for nudging me to go where I was afraid to go in my work & in my heart. And to Maceo Montoya, thank you for opening up your home, your studio, your heart to make my dream your own. You two were my champions through this work, and I am most grateful.

Acknowledgments

The Alfredo Cisneros del Moral Foundation & The Artist Foundation of San Antonio for grants that allowed me to focus solely on my writing during this most difficult season. And the following individuals who offered their cities & homes so that I could think & write & remember: Krystal Bosveld & Chelsea Charvat, Jennifer Barnard, Deborah Paredes, Cindy Hueyser & Deb Winegarten, Liz Cerda-Majeski, Larissa Mercado-López, Margarito, Sylvia, & Berenice Guzmán, Juan Morales, Alejandra Pérez, Malaquías & Lezlie Montoya, Joseph Ríos & Mama Jo & Grandpa Joe, Virginia Grise, and Sandra Cisneros.

As always, thank you, David Garcés, for your unwavering support. And to Drew, Vic, & Liv for being strong enough to fight your way through as best you could, for staying strong for me & for each other. This has been a year of great change. One constant: my love for you.

And my mom & stepdad, Sylvia & Pete Rodríguez, for all your support during this hardest year.

And to my dad & brother, George & Gabriel Guerrero, for knowing all the stories grandpa wouldn't tell me (and for telling me) and for loving me the way I thought only he could.

And thank you, Eloisa, for every single year. *Laurie Ann*

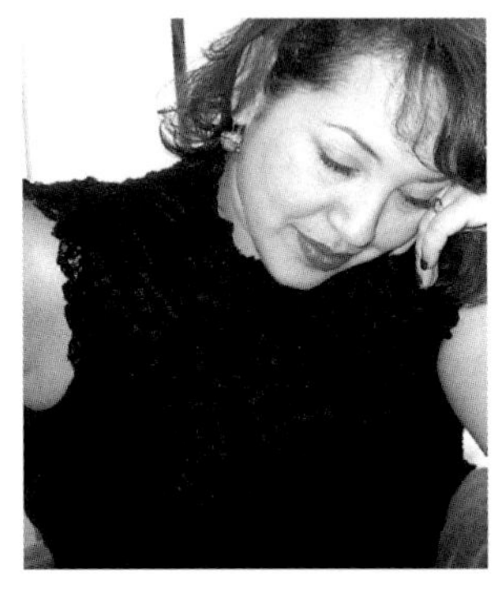

Laurie Ann Guerrero was born and raised in the Southside of San Antonio and was named by former mayor, Julián Castro, Poet Laureate of the City of San Antonio in 2014. Winner of the 2012 Andrés Montoya Poetry Prize, her first full-length collection, *A Tongue in the Mouth of the Dying*, was selected by Francisco X. Alarcón and published by University of Notre Dame Press in 2013. Guerrero's chapbook, *Babies under the Skin* (Panhandler Publishing, 2007), won the Panhandler Chapbook Award, chosen by Naomi Shihab Nye. Guerrero is the recipient of the International Latino Book Award, Alfredo Cisneros del Moral Award, the Academy of American Poets Prize from Smith College, among others. *Poets & Writers Magazine* named Guerrero one of 10 top debut poets in 2014 and *A Tongue in the Mouth of the Dying* was listed as one of 14 must-read works of Chicano literature by Rigoberto González. Guerrero holds a B.A. in English Language & Literature from Smith College and an MFA in Poetry from Drew University. She is the inaugural Poet-in-Residence at Palo Alto College in San Antonio and lives & writes in her hometown.

Maceo Montoya grew up in Elmira, California. He graduated from Yale University in 2002 and received his Master of Fine Arts in painting from Columbia University in 2006. His paintings, drawings, and prints have been featured in exhibitions and publications throughout the country as well as internationally. Montoya's first novel, *The Scoundrel and the Optimist* (Bilingual Review, 2010), was awarded the 2011 International Latino Book Award for "Best First Book" and *Latino Stories* named him one of its "Top Ten New Latino 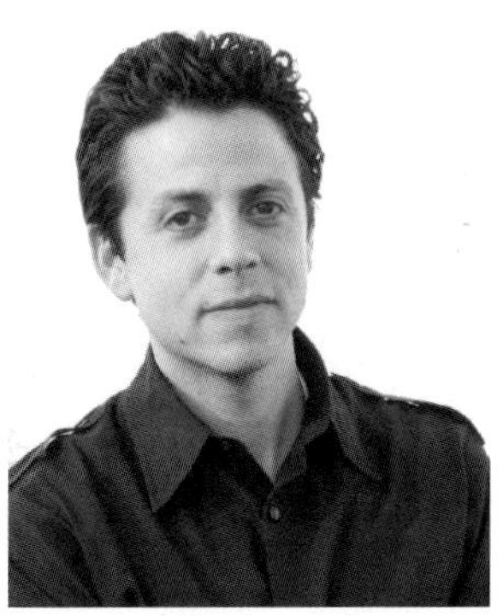 Writers to Watch." In 2014, University of New Mexico Press published his second novel, *The Deportation of Wopper Barraza*, and Copilot Press published *Letters to the Poet from His Brother*, a hybrid book combining images, prose poems, and essays. Montoya is an Assistant Professor in the Chicana/o Studies Department at UC Davis where he teaches the Chicana/o Mural Workshop and courses in Chicano Literature. He is also affiliated with Taller Arte del Nuevo Amanecer (TANA), a community-based arts organization located in Woodland, CA.

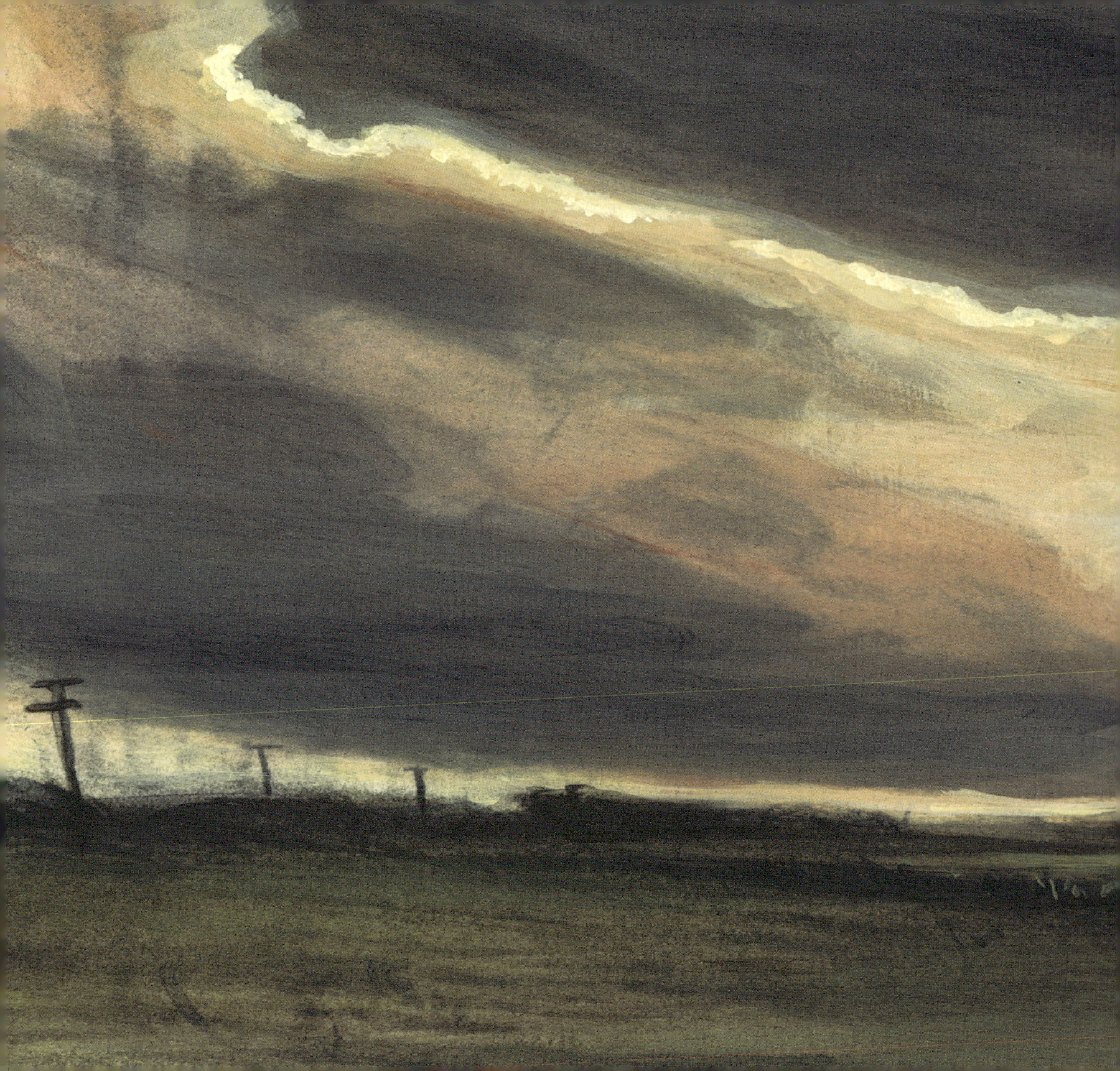